Essential Events

# The Bolshevik Revolution

by Joseph R. O'Neill

Essential Events

# The Bolshevik Revolution

by Joseph R. O'Neill

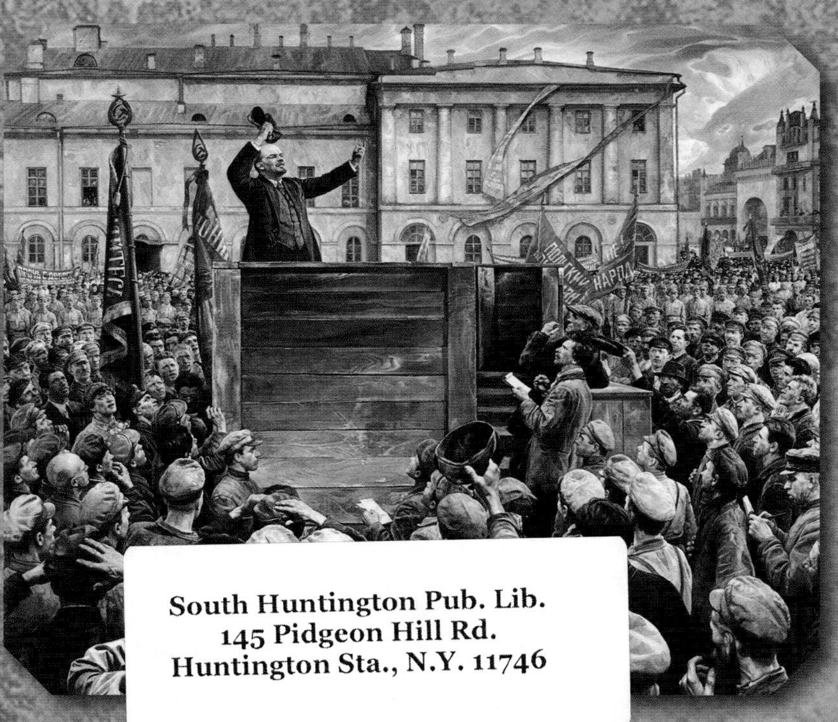



**Content Consultant**
Susan Zayer Rupp
Associate Professor of History
Wake Forest University

**ABDO**
Publishing Company

# CREDITS

Published by ABDO Publishing Company, 8000 West 78th Street, Edina, Minnesota 55439. 

Printed in the United States.

Editor: Paula Lewis
Copy Editor: Nadia Higgins
Interior Design and Production: Rebecca Daum
Cover Design: Rebecca Daum

**Library of Congress Cataloging-in-Publication Data**
O'Neill, Joseph R.
The Bolshevik Revolution / by Joseph R. O'Neill.
p. cm.
Includes bibliographical references and index.
ISBN 978-1-60453-511-2
1. Russia—Politics and government—1894-1917—Juvenile literature. 2. Soviet Union—History—Revolution, 1917-1921—Juvenile literature. I. Title.
DK262.O65 2009
947.084'1—dc22

2008033104

# TABLE OF CONTENTS

Chapter 1

*Tsar Nicholas II with Tsarina Alexandra and their children*

# The End of a Dynasty

Late at night on July 16, 1918, in the Siberian town of Ekaterinburg, Russia, the doctor heard a frantic knock at the door. Yakov Yurovsky, commander of a brigade of secret police, told the doctor to wake the sleeping family. They needed to be rushed to the cellar for their safety. The crackle of gunfire and the roar of artillery could be heard—an army was fighting its way into Ekaterinburg!

Doctor Eugene Botkin was the physician attending the Romanovs—Russia's royal family. For the past 16 months, Botkin and three servants had been held captive in the Siberian town with the emperor of Russia, Tsar Nicholas II, and his wife and five children.

The royal family quickly dressed and followed the guard out of their apartments and down 28 steps into a cellar. The room was empty. There was not even a chair for 13-year-old Alexis, who was stricken with hemophilia. As the tsar's only son, Alexis was the tsarevich—and next in line for the throne.

The young tsarevich's mother, Tsarina Alexandra, requested chairs—one for her ill son and one for herself. The family gathered together, and chairs were brought in for the tsarina and the tsarevich. Tsar Nicholas II stood in front of his son, Alexis, as if he were protecting him. The tsar's four daughters, Olga, Tatiana, Maria, and Anastasia, were the grand duchesses of Russia. They stood next to their mother, and the youngest daughter, Anastasia, cradled her little dog, Jemmy. Doctor Botkin and the family's butler, maid, and cook stood by the Romanovs.

Yurovsky informed the royal family that the Soviet of Workers' Deputies wanted them killed. The family immediately understood what was about to happen. As Yurovsky would later write to his superiors in Moscow, there were "no tears, no sobs, no questions."[1] The gunmen were under his command. Each had been told in advance who his target would be. The men were instructed to aim for the heart, so as not to leave too much blood.

Yurovsky addressed Tsar Nicholas, "In view of the fact that your relatives are continuing their attack on Soviet Russia, the Ural Executive Committee has decided to execute you."[2] With that, Yurovsky shot the tsar, and the 11 other men opened fire.

The tsar and tsarina, the Grand Duchess Olga, Doctor Botkin, the butler, and the cook died instantly. However, the young tsarevich, the maid, and the three younger duchesses survived. Bullets fired at the girls bounced off and ricocheted around the room in a shower

**Tsar**

The Russians used the word *tsar* to refer to the supreme ruler of an empire. Tsar derives from Caesar—the family name of the first emperors of ancient Rome.

of sparks that terrified the assassins. They were unaware that the tsarina had sewn diamonds into her daughters' dresses to hide the jewels from their captors. The stone-hard jewels repelled the gunfire. But the men kept reloading and firing their guns until, at long last, the girls fell.

The assassins repeatedly kicked and stabbed the tsarevich until Yurovsky fired two shots into the boy's ear. The maid, Anna Demidova, was also hiding Russian royal jewels that she had sewn into a pillow she carried for the

**The Romanovs**

In 1613, Mikhail Romanov was crowned tsar of Russia. This marked the beginning of the Romanov dynasty and a period of stability.

During the seventeenth century, the Romanov tsars strengthened their position and solidified the Russian caste system. This system organized society into rigid groups based on social and economic class. A 1649 code of law divided society into categories based on occupations. This made it rare for an individual—and his or her descendants—to leave their assigned category. The law also forbade movement into or out of cities and towns. This policy succeeded in freezing Russian society and gave absolute power to the tsar.

Peter the Great reigned from 1682 to 1725. He opened Russia to Europe, reformed the economy, modernized the military, and centralized the government.

Catherine the Great reigned from 1762 to 1796. Poland and Ukraine were added to the Russian Empire. She encouraged Western cultural and political values among the educated elite. But millions of Russian peasants struggled in lives full of hardship.

It was not until 1861 that Alexander II issued laws that freed the serfs of the Russian Empire. By 1917, the Russian Empire would erupt in revolution and the Romanov monarchy would fall.

The house in Ekaterinburg, Russia, where the Romanov family was held hostage for 16 months

tsarina. Demidova was stabbed 30 times with a dull bayonet.

The victims were dragged out of the cellar and tossed into the back of an awaiting truck. Tsar Nicholas was the first to be dumped in. But one of the girls cried out. Seventeen-year-old Anastasia was still alive. The men descended on the girl, beating her and stabbing her again and again until they were sure that she could no longer possibly be alive. She was thrown onto the truck with the bodies of her family.

As the truck was about to pull away to carry off the bodies of Russia's royal family, a soldier found Anastasia's dog. The soldier viciously smashed the little dog's head with the butt of his gun and tossed it in with the bodies of the royal family. The men climbed on board, and the truck drove off into the night. The killers removed the victims' clothes, which were to be burned. In the process, they recovered more than 17 pounds (8 kg) of jewels. These precious stones included diamonds, rubies, emeralds, and sapphires. After the bodies of the royal family were disfigured with acid, they were burned and buried in a secret location deep in a Siberian forest. Yakov Yurovsky wanted to ensure that no one would ever find out what had happened to the Romanovs.

## The Bolsheviks

The orders for capturing, hiding, and murdering the Romanov family had come from Moscow. A new ruling party in Russia called themselves the Bolsheviks. Unlike the royal family, they claimed to represent working people—the peasant farmers and urban factory workers of Russia. The Bolsheviks had come to power in October 1917.

Vladimir Lenin felt that the Bolshevik government was in danger of collapsing. Lenin's grab for power would result in a civil war. And it was an anti-Bolshevik army that marched toward Ekaterinburg on the night of the royal family's death. Lenin feared the troops would find the royal family, set them free, and return them to power. He could not allow that to happen—the Bolshevik Revolution must be preserved at all costs. Lenin denied the whereabouts of the royal family and ordered their execution to ensure the Romanovs could not return to power.

Lenin's message to all Russians was that the Bolshevik Revolution was in progress. There would be no turning back.

**Anastasia?**

After the murder of the royal family, rumors persisted that Anastasia had escaped and fled. Less than two years later, Anna Anderson claimed that she was Anastasia and had survived the assassination attempt. She filed several unsuccessful lawsuits in an attempt to receive some of the Romanov fortune.

Anna Anderson died in 1984. However, deoxyribonucleic acid (DNA) tests conducted in 1991 concluded that Anna Anderson could not have been related to the Romanov family.

*Tsar Nicholas as painted by Ernst Karlovitch Lipgart, ca. 1900*

Chapter 2

Peasant workers in a field

# The Old Regime

When Nicholas was crowned in 1894, upon his father's death, he had very little experience in government. Yet he was expected to rule the vast expanse of Russia and its territories in Eastern Europe and Central Asia. Nicholas inherited a nation without legal political parties, a parliament, or any elected officials.

There were four social classes, or legal castes, called estates. Every Russian belonged to one of these castes: noble, clergy, townsman, or peasant. And each caste served a specific role in society. Only those who were nobles at birth or attained noble status through service to the state were allowed to fill government posts. The Russian Orthodox Church was the country's national religion. The clergy served the tsar by reinforcing the notion that God had placed him over all Russians as their unquestioned monarch. Townsmen, a small minority of Russians, worked in traditional urban trades or as craftsmen and artisans. The overwhelming majority of Russians—by some estimates, more than 80 percent—belonged to the peasant caste and worked the land.

## Tied to the Land

Until 1861, Russia had been a feudal society. Although some peasants were free and owned small farms of their own, a great many toiled on lands belonging to the nobility. These peasants—called serfs—were bought and sold along with the land they farmed. They had no civil or personal rights.

In return for working for the nobility, they farmed a portion of land to grow their food. In 1861, serfs were officially emancipated, or freed, from their life of service, but their lives did not improve. The former serfs, although now legally free, were still bound to the land. They were given land they had farmed for generations. However, they had to repay their former landlords over a period of 49 years.

## Industrial Expansion

Although Russia was considered to be one of the great powers of Europe, it was socially and technologically behind the industrial nations of the United Kingdom, France, and Germany. Peasants lived in one-room huts clustered along the main roads. They farmed common strips of land using wooden plows. Agricultural techniques common in parts of Europe and in North America were unknown across the expanse of Russia.

Near the turn of the twentieth century, Russia experienced a rapid industrial expansion—some 150 years after Britain and 70 years after France had industrialized. The government encouraged industrialization and helped cities fund the modern factories for large-scale production. These cities included St. Petersburg and Moscow in Russia, Kiev and Odessa in Ukraine, and Warsaw in Poland. Industrialization enabled Russia to begin large-scale production with relatively little effort and fewer industrial growing pains. Russia's new factories soon became competitive with factories in the West. This led to a rapid growth in the prosperity of some skilled workers and the creation of an urban industrial working class.

However, this new urban working class had no legal caste. Unlike the traditional

**Tsar Nicholas II**

Nicholas Alexandrovich Romanov was born on May 6, 1868. He was the eldest son of Tsar Alexander III and Tsarina Maria Fyodorovna. When Nicholas finished his education, he traveled and enjoyed himself. His position as tsarevich was to patiently await his father's death, which most people thought was years away. However, in 1894, when Nicholas was 26, his father died of kidney failure. Nicholas was crowned Tsar Nicholas II. He married the woman he loved, the German Princess Alix.

A granddaughter of England's Queen Victoria, Princess Alix was raised and educated in Britain. Before her marriage to Nicholas, she converted to the Russian Orthodox faith and changed her name to Alexandra Fyodorovna.

Nicholas and Alexandra had four daughters and one son, Alexis. Born in 1904, Alexis had hemophilia, which meant his blood was unable to clot. He could bleed profusely from any cut or bruise, resulting in serious injury or even death. His painful illness caused his mother to bring the mystic healer Rasputin into the royal family's lives.

The citizens of Russia revolted in early 1917, forcing Tsar Nicholas II to abdicate on March 15, 1917. Nicholas and his family were placed under arrest in the remote Siberian town of Ekaterinburg, where they were murdered with their servants on July 16, 1918.

**Trans-Siberian Railroad**

Russia's rapid program of industrialization led to a major push to link St. Petersburg with the Pacific Ocean. Railways already operated from St. Petersburg to Moscow, but the new railway would be far longer, essentially crossing the vast country from east to west. In 1891, construction began on the first leg of the Trans-Siberian Railroad. This included the 1,243 miles (2,000 km) from Moscow to Chelyabinsk in southwestern Siberia. In 1892, construction began at Chelyabinsk and Vladivostok. Located on the Pacific, Vladivostok was the end of the line. The two tracks linked up in 1904.

The railroad proved vital for Russia's industrial expansion. It also was an efficient way to transport soldiers or prisoners bound for exile in Siberia. The world's longest railroad covers 5,777 miles (9,297 km) and is still in use today.

townspeople, these workers had no place in Russia's social class structure. Most of the industrial workers had come to the factories from the farms. After the 1861 emancipation of the serfs, millions of young men left the farms as seasonal workers to earn money throughout the year in Russia's new factories and foundries. The money they earned was sent back to their villages to help pay tax bills and rents. As Russia continued to industrialize, some peasants gave up farming to work in the city.

Their new lives often were no easier than their old lives. Conditions in the factories were terrible. The hours were long, the wages low, and the work was dirty and often dangerous. Children as young as five worked alongside their mothers and fathers for 70 hours a week. In the United States and Western Europe, factory workers fought to form labor unions.

However, Russian workers had no legal rights. They resented their miserable living and working conditions. The Russian monarchy was only interested in keeping up production. It was willing to use the army and police to put down any protests against poor working conditions.

## An Incompetent Government

Not only was Russia's economy outdated, but the government was incompetent. The tsar was the absolute ruler of Russia. This meant that the tsar had total control over the government and that he was above the law. The administration of the empire was in the hands of a select group of noblemen. One's birth status, and not one's talents or experience, was the determining factor for government employment. The military and the foreign service were the responsibility of a few distant cousins of the tsar. Oftentimes, relatives were given promotions to important government posts as favors or presents, regardless of their experience and ability. The tsar was a revered figure, but he did little in the way of central government administration.

Nevertheless, the Russian army was a source of national pride, and the sheer number of

**Russia**

Russia is the world's largest nation and covers more than 10 percent of Earth's landmass. Nearly twice the size of the United States, the country spans 11 time zones and nearly half of the circumference of the world.

Russia sits astride the continents of Europe and Asia. Most of Russia's cities and population are in European Russia. Most of Russian land lies in Asia. This includes Siberia, an area larger than Canada. Most of Siberia experiences winters that last six to eight months with long periods of darkness and extreme temperatures.

In 2007, the population of Russia was 141.4 million—less than half the population of the United States.

troops the tsar could muster was impressive. However, foolish foreign policy decisions and incompetent commanders led to a series of humiliating defeats for the Russian Army. In 1854, Russia had lost the Crimean War against Great Britain, France, the Ottoman Empire (modern Turkey), and Piedmont-Sardinia. Several horrendous blunders cost tens of thousands of lives and forced the Russians to sign the humiliating Treaty of Paris in 1856. As a condition of the treaty, Russia lost control of the Black Sea, which then became a neutral territory. The myth of Russian strength was exposed, and Russia lost some of its territory to the Ottoman Empire.

In 1904, Japan launched a sneak attack against the Russians in retaliation over Russian activities in Manchuria (China) and Korea. The Russians suffered heavy casualties as Japan's modern warships crushed Russia's aging fleet.

This painting depicts the Japanese destruction of Russian warships in the Russo-Japanese War of 1904 and 1905.

After 18 months of fighting, both countries agreed to the Treaty of Portsmouth. The treaty was mediated by U.S. President Theodore Roosevelt. This marked the beginning of the United States as a power in world diplomacy.

## Growing Discontent

Dissatisfaction with the absolute monarchy in Russia had been simmering since the 1820s. However, Nicholas's government of the late nineteenth century and early twentieth century was particularly incompetent and inefficient. His government inspired revolutionary activities to a degree never before seen in Russian history. By the early twentieth century, a mystic healer held influence over the royal family. Food was scarce in St. Petersburg. Tsar Nicholas was often absent from the capital, conducting a war against Germany. Millions of young Russian soldiers were dying because of inept commanders.

By 1917, the people were ready for change. Hundreds of thousands of workers took to the streets to protest. Revolution was at hand. But to what direction would a new Russia turn? What would a post-tsarist Russia look like, and who would lead the country?

*Peasants outside a log house, ca. 1909*

Chapter 3

*The coronation of Tsar Nicholas II and Tsarina Alexandra*

# New Ideas

In the early nineteenth century, many Russians had come in contact with the values and political philosophies of the Western world. Many were left with a taste for personal liberty. On December 14, 1825, a group of Russian officers, later known as the Decembrists, staged an unsuccessful uprising against Tsar Nicholas I. Their goal was to remove the absolutist tsar from power. Instead, their failure ensured another 90 years of tyranny. However, their actions did compel Tsar Nicholas I to turn his attention to some of Russia's problems. Although he refused to free the serfs, he made some attempts to improve the lives of state-owned serfs. However, Nicholas I was more intent on suppressing revolutionary ideas than improving the lives of his subjects.

## Growing Unrest

Between 1825 and 1854, nearly 500 peasant revolts erupted across Russia. In 1853, the imperial ambitions of Tsar Nicholas I to gain access to the Mediterranean led to the Crimean War. However, the tsar died in 1855, one year before the conclusion of the war. His son, Tsar Alexander II, was left to face defeat at the hands of the British and French. The general dissatisfaction of the Russian people was fueled by the humiliating losses in the Crimean War.

Ultimately, Tsar Alexander II was forced to initiate a series of reforms to ensure Russia's place as a world power. These reforms included the abolition of serfdom, the relaxation of censorship laws, and the construction of hospitals and schools. Rural towns and districts were given the power to govern themselves and collect taxes. Emancipation was not a simple matter of granting land to the peasants. In an effort to prevent too much change from happening too quickly, the system for freeing the serfs was made complicated. This kept the serfs bound to the land. This and other failed attempts of land reform further aggravated the Russian people.

Some groups turned to violence to achieve reforms that would help the people. Tsar Alexander II was shot at in 1866 and again in 1876. In 1879, the royal train was blown up. The tsar narrowly escaped each assassination attempt. In 1880, the People's Will blew up the banquet hall in the tsar's Winter Palace. On March 1, 1881, Nicholas Rysakov tossed a bomb at the royal carriage. Debris and wreckage scattered everywhere, but the tsar survived the initial blast. Ignacy Grinevitsky tossed a second bomb. Tsar Alexander II was mortally wounded and died later that evening.

Rysakov and Grinevitsky were members of the radical group that called itself the People's Will. The group hoped to stir the masses into open revolt and terrify the government into submission. However, their plan backfired. The next tsar of Russia, Alexander III, reacted by ruthlessly crushing any anti-tsarist movements—terrorist or not. Furthermore, the people were disgusted with the murderous tactics of the People's Will. When Tsar Alexander III died of natural causes in 1894, his son became Tsar Nicholas II.

In 1904, anger over the heavy and humiliating losses to the smaller Japanese fleet in the Russo-Japanese War led to nationwide protests and work stoppages. Vyacheslav Plehve, the minister of the interior and director of the state police, ruthlessly cracked down on the popular demonstrations. Plehve's actions, in turn, led to more intense anger and hatred toward the government. Ultimately, Plehve was assassinated in July 1904.

## Bloody Sunday

Father Georgi Gapon had organized labor unions in St. Petersburg as part of his missionary work. On January 9, 1905, Father Gapon harnessed the anger of the St. Petersburg masses. He led more than 120,000 workers in a peaceful march to the Winter Palace to petition the tsar for labor

*A depiction of the first day of the Russian Revolution (January 9, 1905), known as Bloody Sunday, as painted by Vladimir Egorovich Makovsky*

reform. The marchers peacefully carried religious icons and pro-tsarist banners. They sang patriotic and religious songs, as if they were taking part in a religious procession. The solemn procession wound through St. Petersburg's streets without incident. But when the marchers reached the Winter Palace, they were met with armed guards. The troops ordered the crowd to disperse and then opened fire. Approximately 130 people were killed and several hundred were wounded. The massacre came to be known as Bloody Sunday. It served as a rallying cry for revolutionaries across Russia.

The Russian public reacted to news of the event with disgust and outrage. People with varying political views denounced the killings. Public outrage once again spilled into the streets. Riots, looting, lockouts, and mass strikes crippled the capital. The royal family's response was to wait out the violence.

## The Tsar's Answer

Seven months later, in order to pacify the mobs, Nicholas announced the formation of a national assembly, called the Imperial Duma. However, the tsar's proposed duma was not enough to soothe the anti-tsarist feelings of the Russian people. The working class, peasants, and the hundreds of non-Russian ethnic groups were given a minor representation in the Imperial Duma. Furthermore, the powers promised to the Imperial Duma fell short of what the liberals and radicals desired. The people reacted negatively to this meager attempt at reform. There were more strikes and protests.

From August through October 1905, many vital industries were shut down. Russia was becoming paralyzed. On October 17, 1905, under pressure from the nobility, the tsar signed the October Manifesto. This manifesto promised personal liberty and freedom of the press and assembly. It also promised universal voting rights and the formation of a representative assembly—the State Duma. The tsar retained control of the church and the appointment of governmental ministers.

The people were elated. However, when representatives made demands for land reforms and the release of political prisoners, Nicholas rejected these demands. The tsar had no intention of keeping promises he had been forced to sign. On July 8, 1906, only three months after the State Duma had first convened, Tsar Nicholas dissolved the assembly and filled it with men who were loyal to him. By suppressing the popular discontent, the tsarist government was about to reassert much of its power. It also withdrew many of the concessions granted in 1905.

**Monarchies**

In 1917, Russia was an absolute monarchy in which the tsar could act without interference.

## The Intelligentsia

Long before terrorist groups such as the People's Will, others had been interested in governmental reform. Some nobles were sympathetic to the plight of the masses. Those who had the luxury of a European education and were familiar with Western philosophies and ideals also desired change in Russia. These reformists comprised a group called the intelligentsia—with two viewpoints.

One side favored a constitutional liberal democracy. The other side strongly disliked the individualistic ideals typical of the West. This group considered themselves Slavophiles. They felt that Russians and other Slavs were of a unique culture based on the Russian Orthodox Church and communal village life.

Upper-class Russians favored some westernizing philosophies. They envisioned a modernization of the monarchy similar to the monarchy of Great Britain. The Slavophiles desired a representative assembly—a parliament or senate—that worked with the tsar to create laws and direct national policy. Rather than forcing change through violence, they favored petitioning the tsar to implement constitutional changes.

## To the People

In the mid-nineteenth century, political writer Alexander Herzen called for the elimination of the monarchy. He idealized what he believed to be the simple and pure life of the Russian peasant. He believed that an empowered peasantry would result in a revolution from the bottom up. The old system, in which wealth was in the hands of a very few, would be overturned.

By the 1860s and 1870s, a view that came to be known as Populism (Narodnichestvo) emerged. Russian Populists believed that capitalist industrialization had ruined Europe and led to the degradation of humans. Populists also believed that capitalism was not only inherently selfish, but that it led to the disintegration of society. In contrast, they saw the peasant communities as societies that promoted equality. If nurtured, these societies would expand and lead to a Slavic utopian society for everyone.

However, the Populists were generally from the upper-middle class. Many had been educated only in France or Germany. Most were

**Capitalism**

The private ownership of farms, factories, and businesses and the sale of goods and services for profit is known as capitalism.

Those promoting a revolution spoke against capitalism and promised equality for all.

unfamiliar with the customs of their birth country and even had to learn the Russian language. They had never worked the land and had an idealized concept of the agrarian life. Narodnichestvo was unsuccessful and aroused the suspicion of the peasants and the police.

## Action, Not Deliberation

Sergei Nechayev, Mikhail Bakunin, and Peter Tkachev were the forerunners of Lenin and the Bolsheviks. Nechayev advocated political violence and methods of terror and disinformation to overthrow the old system. Bakunin supported terrorism to destroy the entire structure of tsarist Russia. Tkachev believed that a rational discussion of a new direction for Russia was beyond the intelligence of most people and a waste of time. He advocated immediate and violent action.

These three activists spread their message of violent revolution to the peasant masses throughout Russia. The embarrassing failure of "going to the people" gave credibility to the view that the common masses were not capable of understanding and unwilling to execute a revolution. Therefore, the intellectuals would create a revolution for them.

## Marxism

Marxists were members of the intelligentsia who favored the writings of Karl Marx, a German philosopher. Marx believed that all of human history was the story of struggle between the classes—the haves and the have-nots. For centuries, serfs tilled the soil and harvested crops for the elite. Eventually, peasants moved into the cities and began working for middle-class businessmen—the bourgeoisie—in their shops and small factories. The bourgeoisie grew wealthy and controlled production. This included farms, factories, foundries, and mines.

Over time, a majority of the population settled in big cities and worked in the factories. Marx called these urban factory workers and the laboring class the proletariat. They performed dirty and dangerous work for long hours and little pay. Marx believed that the proletariat was enslaved as were the slaves of the American South. Although a factory worker was "free" to quit his job, Marx would argue that the worker would have been left destitute, tossed out of society, and unable to survive in a world controlled by the bourgeoisie.

Religion also played a role in the capitalist world. Marx argued that by teaching it is noble and good to suffer in the eyes of God, the church kept people in their humble position.

Marx predicted the nobility would be overthrown by the bourgeoisie. Capitalism would flourish and the peasants would overthrow the bourgeoisie. The factories and farms would become the common property of all people. Everyone would work for the collective goal and produce only what they needed. They would be a society without nobility, bourgeoisie, church, money, or markets.

Many Russian revolutionaries adapted Marx's teachings. But Marxist ideas did not fit well with the reality of Russia.

**Karl Marx**

Karl Marx was born on May 5, 1818, in Germany. He studied at the University of Bonn and the University of Berlin. In 1842, Marx became the editor of a newspaper in Cologne. He was asked to leave the paper one year later because his articles were critical of German society and politics. Marx moved to Paris, where he developed his economic and political theories regarding class struggles.

In 1844, Marx was forced to leave France because of his radical political views. He resettled in Brussels, Belgium, and began work on *The Communist Manifesto* with Freidrich Engels. His manifesto explained that revolution was inevitable. Marx predicted an ongoing class struggle between the working class (the proletariat) and those who owned the factories and farms (the bourgeoisie).

Exiled from Brussels in 1848, Marx returned to Cologne. He later settled in London and produced significant political and historical works, including his most famous book, *Das Kapital* (1867). He died in London on March 14, 1883.

> "Society as a whole is more and more splitting up into two great hostile camps, into two great classes directly facing each other: Bourgeoisie and Proletariat."[1]
>
> —*Karl Marx and Friedrich Engels,* The Communist Manifesto

Marx predicted a violent revolution of the urban masses against the capitalist elite. Even though Russia had industrialized at the end of the nineteenth century, the country was an agrarian society—not an urban society. According to Marx, the urban proletariat would be at the forefront of the revolution, not the peasants. He also predicted that the ideal society would follow an era of bourgeois capitalism. However, such an era had not occurred. Russia was still a feudal society. The implementation of Marx's teachings would require skipping the essential step of bourgeois capitalism in the predicted progress of human history.

Despite such problems, the Marxist doctrine that a violent revolution was not only necessary, but inevitable, appealed to Vladimir Ilyich Lenin and Leon Trotsky. It also appealed to others who dreamed of and planned for a bloody Russian revolution.

A sculpture of Karl Marx in Germany

Chapter 4

Portrait of Vladimir Ilyich Lenin

# Lenin and the Bolsheviks

In 1870, Vladimir Ilyich Ulyanov, later to be known as Lenin, was born in Simbirsk, 553 miles (890 km) southeast of Moscow. His father earned a comfortable middle-class income as the director of education of the Simbirsk province, and his mother was a teacher. His father died in 1886 from a cerebral hemorrhage.

On May 8, 1887, when Vladimir Ilyich was 17 years old, five students who had planned the assassination of Tsar Alexander III were publicly hanged. One of those students was Vladimir Ilyich's older brother. Vladimir Ilyich watched as his mother tried to persuade her middle-class friends to aid her son. Vladimir Ilyich was filled with anger at the execution of his brother. He seethed at what he saw as the hypocrisy of his mother's bourgeois friends. They professed their love of freedom and a desire for change but did nothing to prevent Alexander Ilyich's execution.

## A Student and a Revolutionary

Vladimir Ilyich later attended the University of Kazan, where he intended to study law. However, he was expelled after one year for participating in student demonstrations. He moved to his mother's estate near St. Petersburg and studied law at the University of St. Petersburg. He devoured radical literature. He was particularly inspired by *What Is to Be Done?* by Chernyshevsky. The author asserted that personal discipline and a single-minded attention to radical politics were essential to what he termed the "strongman" revolutionary leader. The young student also began distributing Marxist pamphlets around St. Petersburg and using the pseudonym Lenin.

Lenin moved to southeastern Russia and worked as an attorney's assistant. His revolutionary politics limited his options in the legal profession. He devoted his time to radical politics instead. A few months later, Lenin moved to St. Petersburg to pursue the revolutionary cause full time. He became active in Marxist intellectual circles and devoted time to explaining to the working class their potential political power. In 1895, Lenin and his future wife, Nadezhda Krupskaya, were arrested by the tsarist police and sentenced to exile in Siberia.

While in exile, Lenin and Krupskaya spent their time reading and writing. In 1899, Lenin published *The Development of Capitalism in Russia* in which he attempted to formally adapt Marxist theory to Russia. He argued that, although Russia was economically backward, it did fit the mold of a capitalist society. He also argued that while Marx identified the proletariat as the urban working class, Russia's immense peasantry was similarly oppressed by a few wealthy landowners. Lenin believed that Russia was ready for a revolution and the establishment of a utopia run by factory workers and peasants.

In 1900, Lenin moved to Munich, Germany, where he managed the Marxist newspaper *Iskra* (The Spark). The goal of *Iskra* was to unite Russian Marxists in the cause to bring down the Russian monarchy. Lenin did not believe in advancing socialist causes through established channels of government. Rather, Lenin adhered to the

**Lenin's Wife**

Nadezhda Konstantinovna Krupskaya was born in St. Petersburg on February 26, 1869. By the 1890s, she was a committed Marxist. In 1894, she met Vladimir Ilyich Lenin. In 1895, she was arrested by the tsar's secret police for helping Marxists (including Lenin) organize a labor union. Krupskaya was exiled to Siberia for five years. Lenin was also arrested but not sent into exile until after he served a 15-month prison term. In 1898, Lenin and Krupskaya were reunited and married while in exile. They spent much of their time reading and writing revolutionary literature. Lenin was freed from exile in 1900. Two years later, Krupskaya joined him in Germany, and they worked on the Marxist newspaper, *Iskra* (The Spark).

In the 1903 Second Congress of the Russian Socialist Democratic Party, Krupskaya sided with Lenin in the party split that resulted in the Bolsheviks and the Mensheviks. She and Lenin lived in Switzerland until the 1917 overthrow of the tsar. She then worked with Lenin to overthrow the Provisional Government. After the October Revolution, she became the Deputy People's Commissar for Education and Enlightenment.

Lenin died in 1924. Krupskaya published her biography of Lenin, *Reminiscences of Lenin,* in 1933. Nadezhda Konstantinovna Krupskaya died on February 27, 1939.

belief that revolution should arise out of violent action. Lenin felt that Marxists who tried to negotiate with the bourgeois political systems were traitors to the spirit of the Marxist revolution.

## Political Parties

As early as the 1890s, a group of revolutionaries formed the Russian Social Democratic Labor Party (SD). The party united various smaller groups. Their movement centered on Marxist theory. However, they believed that the attainment of the Marxist socialist ideal could occur only after a reorganization of the economy. SD members believed in following Marxist theory to the letter. This meant allowing a capitalist stage of economic development in Russia before the proletarian revolution could occur.

SD members visualized two stages to the revolution. First, the socialists would assist the Russian bourgeoisie in the overthrow of the tsar. They would establish a Western-style liberal democracy with guarantees

***Iskra***

Lenin and Leon Trotsky were among those who worked on *Iskra,* the Marxist newspaper. *Iskra* is Russian for spark. The title came from the phrase: *From a spark a fire will flare up.* The Marxists viewed their revolution as a flame that would encircle the globe, purging the world of the injustices faced by the workers. The Marxist writers of *Iskra* believed that their newspaper would be the spark that would ignite that symbolic fire of revolution.

of personal rights and political freedom. Then, the socialists would take advantage of the guaranteed political freedoms and organize the working classes (the proletariat) to rise up against the bourgeois capitalists. Only then would Russia become a socialist utopia along Marxist lines. Although a Marxist and a leading member of the SD party, Lenin strongly disagreed with this proposed strategy. Lenin believed that Russia was immediately ready for a revolution.

Political parties were illegal in Russia. The first meeting of the SD members (First Congress of the Russian Socialist Democratic Labor Party) was held in 1898. It was broken up by police, and many attendees were jailed. At the Second Congress in 1903, Lenin challenged the SD members to vote on party organization and membership. Lenin argued for an organization of full-time professional revolutionaries. Yuly Martov, another SD party leader and rival to Lenin, argued for a broader membership that was open to anyone who shared the same general Marxist beliefs.

The question of membership and organization was put to a vote, and Lenin's side won a narrow victory. Lenin's party called themselves the Bolsheviks—the majority. Martov's party was called the Mensheviks—the minority. Lenin was determined to become the revolutionary strongman.

A revolutionary rival to the SD party (the Bolsheviks and Mensheviks) sprang up. The Socialist-Revolutionary Party (SR) was a descendant of the violent People's Will organization that had worked to oust the monarchy in 1880. It did not differentiate between the peasants and the proletariat as did the SD party. In the SR's view, both rural and urban classes could be exploited to bring about radical change.

SR members spread their message of revolution and land reform in the villages and countryside. They advocated the elimination of private property. They favored plots of land farmed by a community for the benefit of all members. Because the SR spoke directly to the needs of the peasantry, they had more popular support than the SD. The Bolsheviks and Mensheviks focused primarily on the urban workers.

Lenin spent much of his time strengthening the Bolshevik party. He defended his ideas not only to members of the SR, but also to the Mensheviks—and his Bolshevik rivals.

Nadezhda Krupskaya was a member of the Marxist Socialist Democratic Party and Vladimir Lenin's wife.

Chapter 5

*Austria's Archduke Franz Ferdinand and his wife, Sophie, approach a car moments before the archduke was assassinated on June 28, 1914.*

# World War I and the Russian Revolution

Archduke Franz Ferdinand was the heir to the throne of the Austro-Hungarian Empire in Europe. On June 28, 1914, he was assassinated by a Serbian nationalist in Sarajevo, Bosnia. The Black Hand terrorist group did not want Bosnia to be ruled by the Austro-Hungarian Empire. This murder initiated a series of chain reactions as one nation declared war on another. By August, all of Europe was engulfed in the flames of war.

Russia sided with France and Great Britain. The French and British fought German troops along the Western Front. The Russians fought the Germans and Austrians along the Eastern Front. Initially, Russians reacted to the war with a patriotic surge, expressing their support and love for the tsar and his immense army. The Germanic name of the capital, St. Petersburg, was dropped in favor of the Russian name, Petrograd.

**Autocracy**

The Russian people not only protested the war, they wanted a change in the form of their government.

At this time, Russia had an autocratic government. The political power and decision-making process were held by one person—the tsar.

## Many Losses and Low Morale

However, the war proved to be extremely costly for all involved and especially for Russia. Millions of men died fighting a war that most Russians did not understand. By 1916, Tsar Nicholas II's incompetent leadership had taken its toll. In addition to the losses on the war front, Russian civilians went hungry as poor planning led to food shortages in Petrograd and Moscow. The people were mourning, hungry, and disillusioned.

Between 1914 and 1917, approximately 1.8 million Russian soldiers died. Another 2.8 million soldiers were wounded and 2.4 million were taken as prisoners. Many more civilians died of starvation and disease. The Russians also lost territory. Tsar Nicholas II left the capital for the front lines, where he was giving commands and trying to boost troop morale. By January 1917, German troops were deep into Russia.

## A Country in Crisis

In Petrograd, Tsarina Alexandra had fallen under the spell of Rasputin, a monk who claimed to

**World War I**

World War I began on July 28, 1914. On that day, the Austro-Hungarian Empire declared war on Serbia for the assassination of Archduke Franz Ferdinand. This triggered alliances. Germany declared war on Russia. France and Britain declared war against Germany. The Allied Powers of France, Britain, Russia, other smaller alliances, and eventually the United States, fought the Central Powers of Germany, Austria-Hungary, Bulgaria, and the Ottoman Empire.

Four years after the war began, an armistice was signed on November 11, 1918. Casualties were estimated at 37 million, not including 10 million civilian deaths. The political map of Europe was redrawn. The war's participants were weakened militarily, politically, and economically. In 1919, the Treaty of Versailles was signed. It placed the entire war burden on Germany—an estimated $190 billion—and created the environment in which Adolf Hitler rose to power.

Rasputin reportedly could control the tsarevich's hemophilia.

hold mystical powers. Rasputin claimed he could see into the future and control Alexis's hemophilia. He flaunted his connection to the royal family and his control over the tsarina. Rasputin advised the tsarina to pressure her husband on political appointments. His influence led to the placement of incompetent men in top positions.

Food shortages worsened. Trains that normally would have brought food to market were being used to transport millions of troops. Workers protested the war and the government by refusing to work. In December 1916, a group of noblemen, concerned about the reputation of the royal family, conspired to murder Rasputin. Upon Rasputin's death, Nicholas replaced the incompetent ministers and officers Rasputin had pushed for. However, little could be done to curb the growing discontent. Nicholas was committed to serving as commander-in-

### Rasputin the Mad Monk

Rasputin was born in 1869 in Siberia. An illiterate peasant, he left his village in 1901 as a wandering "holy man" or monk. By 1905, he was at the imperial court. He appeared to be able to control the tsarevich's hemophilia with songs, prayers, and stories. The tsarina was convinced he had magical powers. Rasputin became a trusted advisor to Alexandra.

In 1916, Rasputin urged Alexandra to pressure her husband to appoint Alexander Protopopov as minister of the interior. Protopopov was said to dabble in the occult. Rasputin had gone too far. His influence at court contributed to the shame the Russian nobility already felt about the ruling family's behavior. A group of noblemen plotted to kill Rasputin.

On December 29, 1916, Prince Felix Yusupov invited Rasputin to a party where he was served poisoned cakes and wine. Rasputin showed no ill effects. Prince Felix shot him in the back. Rasputin fell to the floor, but moments later, he stood up. A struggle ensued, and aristocrats shot him several times. Again, he fell to the floor. The noblemen beat Rasputin and dumped him in the Neva River.

Days later, Rasputin's body was discovered. The cause of death was not the poison, the four gunshot wounds, nor the beating. Rasputin drowned trying to claw through the ice of the frozen river.

chief of the Russian troops, and this kept him from returning to the capital.

Throughout January 1917, workers continued to strike and the citizens of Petrograd marched through the streets chanting, "We Want Bread!" While the country was in turmoil, Minister of the Interior Protopopov held séances in the palace. He claimed to raise the spirit of Rasputin in order to convince the tsarina that he could help with the growing crisis.

On February 23, 1917, International Women's Day, an estimated 90,000 men and women textile workers went on strike in Petrograd. Angry about standing in long lines every day for food, the workers chanted, "We Want Bread!" The following day, industrial workers joined the strike. The number of protestors increased greatly and perhaps even doubled. Students and citizens joined in. The crowd also began to chant, "Down with Autocracy, Down with War." Approximately 160,000 soldiers were dispatched to the city to restore order. However, most of the troops refused to fire on their own countrymen—and many joined the protesters.

Duma President Mikhail Vladimirovich Rodzianko sent the following message to Tsar Nicholas, who was still at the war front:

> *Situation is serious. In the capital anarchy. Government is paralyzed. It is essential at once to [entrust] a person enjoying the country's confidence with the formation of government. All delay is death.*[1]

Clearly, Nicholas did not understand the gravity of the situation. He told Rodzianko to end the disorder at once.

Mobs of protesters stormed the prisons and jails. They freed rapists and murderers along with political prisoners. They cut off telephone and telegraph connections. They burned down government buildings as royal ministers fled. Within a few days, the revolutionaries held the railway stations, bridges, artillery depots, and major government buildings. The tsar lost the city.

Tsar Nicholas II officially abdicated power on March 15, 1917. Russia ceased to be a monarchy. The royal family was placed under house arrest outside Petrograd. They were later moved to Ekaterinburg in Siberia.

## A Provisional Government

Initially, Russia was led by a provisional, or temporary, government. The Provisional

Government was formed by as many as one-third of the members of the State Duma. Until elections could be held for a governing body, this assembly, comprised of representatives of the people, would determine the fate of Russia. The Provisional Government granted civil and legal rights to all citizens of Russia, guaranteed freedom of speech and the press, abolished the death penalty, and allowed the return of all political exiles.

However, the Provisional Government did not grant the peasants the land they farmed. They also kept the country in an unpopular war.

Marxist exiles Leon Trotsky and Joseph Stalin returned immediately. Lenin lived in Switzerland, which was a neutral country in World War I. To return to Russia, Lenin needed to cross German lines. However, the Germans realized it was in their best interest to help with Lenin's return to his home country. Lenin was against Russia's participation in the war. Winston Churchill later wrote:

> *. . . with a sense of awe [the Germans] turned upon Russia the most grisly of all weapons. They transported Lenin in a sealed truck [train] like a plague of bacillus from Switzerland into Russia.*[2]

Lenin arrived in Petrograd on April 16, 1917, and was met by cheering crowds. However, Lenin made only a short speech before making his way to Bolshevik headquarters. There was a revolution to plan and execute.

*Leon Trotsky greeted a German officer during a cease-fire on the Russian front.*

Chapter 6

Tsar Nicholas II opens the first Duma.

# The *April Theses* and July Days

In 1905, Nicholas II had been forced to grant concessions to the people and establish a State Duma. Some of these concessions included improving social services and allowing workers to organize. In the wake of peasant rebellions and governmental incompetence, however, there were few leaders able to take on these new efforts. Russia's Marxists stepped in to fill the gap. The Marxists established workers' councils, called soviets, to address workers' grievances and organize the working class for revolutionary activities. Workers, peasants, soldiers, and sailors established soviets across Russia.

In 1905, the St. Petersburg Soviet consisted of 500 delegates representing 250,000 workers. The delegates met to debate the soviet's policy toward revolutionary tactics. The soviet then proclaimed policies by publishing a newspaper and propagandistic pamphlets. Leon Trotsky, who led the soviet, pushed to organize workers into armed militias. At this time, Trotsky was a Menshevik, although he joined the Bolsheviks in 1917 after the February Revolution.

## The Mensheviks and the Provisional Government

After the fall of the tsar in 1917, power was in the hands of the Provisional Government. It entered a short-lived power-sharing arrangement with the Petrograd Soviet.

The Provisional Government was determined to shepherd Russia toward a liberal democracy. This goal was supported by the majority of Mensheviks in the Petrograd Soviet. They believed a liberal bourgeois democracy would bring about an era of Russian capitalism—a necessary step on the path to their ultimate goal. The capitalist system would then be overthrown by the proletariat in order to establish a workers' socialist paradise.

The Provisional Government relied upon the support of the soviet. The workers' group had shown its power during the chaotic events of the February uprising. During that time, members of the soviet militia kept the city from totally collapsing. They ran many telephone and telegraph stations, post offices, and railway depots.

**City Names**

St. Petersburg was the tsarist capital of Russia. At the outbreak of World War I, the city's name was changed to Petrograd. After Lenin's death in 1924, Petrograd was renamed Leningrad, in honor of the late Bolshevik leader. The city was renamed St. Petersburg again in 1991 after the collapse of the Soviet Union.

## The Bolsheviks and the Provisional Government

When Lenin returned to Petrograd in 1917, he pushed for control. He was opposed to the war and the Provisional Government. Most Mensheviks in the Petrograd Soviet backed the Provisional Government. Lenin persuaded the Bolsheviks to denounce the Provisional Government and work toward its overthrow. The Provisional Government still supported Russia's involvement in the war.

## The *April Theses*

In June 1917, the Petrograd Soviet hosted the All-Russia Congress of Soviets of Workers' and Soldiers' Deputies. Lenin read his *April Theses* that urged the soviets of Russia to withdraw all support for the Provisional Government. He condemned the war and demanded Russia's immediate withdrawal. Lenin also denounced the formation of a liberal democracy. He believed that Russia had already progressed through a capitalist stage and that the time was ripe for a proletariat revolution. Lenin envisioned a government as a republic of workers' soviets instead of a representative democracy. Finally, Lenin stated that the workers' revolution would not be limited to Russia. It was not a matter of Russian politics or social problems. The socialist revolution would be an international phenomenon.

Lenin's *April Theses* characterized his revolutionary style. The tone was belligerent and uncompromising. He advocated crushing anyone or anything that hindered the revolution. Lenin compared the workers of the world to a giant iron broom that would sweep away all signs of the middle class. He expected the working class to use violent methods to seize factories, banks, and farms.

In the coming months, Lenin tirelessly continued

**The *April Theses***

Lenin's *April Theses* called for the soviets to seize power and take control. Specifically, he called for:

> *. . . a transition from the first stage of revolution . . . to its second stage which is to place the power in the hands of the proletariat and the . . . peasantry. . . .*
>
> *No support to the Provisional Government. . . .*
>
> *It must be explained to the masses that the Soviet of Workers' Deputies is the only possible form of revolutionary government. . . .*
>
> *Not a parliamentary republic . . . but a republic of Soviets of Workers', Agricultural Labourers' and Peasants' Deputies. . . .*
>
> *Abolition of the police, the army. . . . All officers to be elected . . . their salaries not to exceed the average wage of a competent worker. . . .*
>
> *Confiscation of private lands. . . .*
>
> *. . . the Soviet of Workers' Deputies [to be] in control of social production and distribution of goods. . . .*[1]

to preach his message of destruction and violent revolution to the people of Russia. The Bolsheviks organized mass protests and strikes. They convinced the people that the food shortages and war with Germany were the fault of the inept and corrupt bourgeois Provisional Government. Popular dissatisfaction with the war intensified. Marchers carried banners emblazoned with "All Power to the Soviets!"

## The Collapse of the Bolsheviks

In July, tensions exploded with massive street demonstrations, workers' strikes, and military defections. This time of unrest came to be known as the July Days. Alexander Kerensky, the head of the Provisional Government, viewed these events as a Bolshevik attempt to overthrow the Provisional Government. Kerensky responded to the protests with force and ordered the arrest of prominent Bolshevik leaders.

Trotsky was arrested and briefly sent to prison. Disguised, Lenin

**The Smolny Institute**

During 1917, the Smolny Institute in Petrograd served as the headquarters of the Bolshevik party. Before that, the building had been a school for daughters of nobles. With the political turmoil in Petrograd, the school was not used. After the overthrow of the tsar, the Bolsheviks took it over. Lenin ruled Russia from the institute until 1918, when he moved his base to Moscow.

*Fighting erupted outside the Duma between Lenin's and Kerensky's supporters.*

escaped to Finland. The Bolsheviks lost face during the July Days. They simply were unprepared and collapsed under the pressure.

## A Nation in Chaos

German forces marched closer and closer to Petrograd. Russian patriotism temporarily recovered, and the people rallied to the defense of their capital. Lenin's return to Russia in April had been aided by the Germans and exploited by his enemies. They labeled Lenin as a German secret agent. The Bolsheviks had been silenced.

Law and order was decaying in the capital. The Provisional Government was unable to provide even basic services to the Russian people. By late August, General Lavr Georgiyevich Kornilov took military action to remedy the situation. Kornilov intended to restore order and strengthen Kerensky's Provisional Government. His plan called for dismantling the soviets and hanging the Bolsheviks. But instead of gratitude, Kerensky ordered Kornilov to step down. Kornilov ordered his troops to occupy Petrograd. General Kornilov was accused of mounting a coup and placed under arrest.

Kerensky tried to move ahead with the formation of a Constituent Assembly. He organized a temporary pre-parliament that would later be

**Alexander Kerensky**

Alexander Kerensky was a member of the Socialist-Revolutionary Party (SR). After the 1917 February Revolution, Kerensky served as minister of justice of the Provisional Government. In April, he became minister of war and continued the war against the Central Powers. By the end of June, Kerensky had become prime minister of the Provisional Government. Kerensky's government had lofty ambitions, but its efforts were unsuccessful. By October, Russia's downward spiral—begun under the rule of Nicholas—was as steep as ever.

Lenin then orchestrated the Bolshevik Revolution that overthrew the Provisional Government. Kerensky tried to rally Russian troops to help restore the Provisional Government, but his men failed to act. Kerensky fled to Paris. Later, he moved to New York City, where he died on June 11, 1970.

replaced by an established parliament. Kerensky was determined to establish a liberal democracy in Russia. The pre-parliament met on October 20, 1917, with 550 delegates. However, Trotsky and other Bolshevik delegates stormed out of the meeting, denouncing what they called the bourgeois capitalist democracy.

Meanwhile, disguised in a red wig and a long overcoat, Lenin left Finland and returned unnoticed to Petrograd. He made a surprise visit to the Bolshevik central committee. He told his fellow Bolsheviks that this was the time for an armed overthrow of the bourgeois Provisional Government.

During the July Days of 1917, Petrograd workers were urged to support the actions against the Provisional Government.

Chapter 7

Alexander Kerensky (in a 1938 photo) was the prime minister of Russia's Provisional Government in June 1917.

# Red October

After Lenin's surprise visit to the Bolshevik central committee, plans for an armed revolution began. Trotsky formed the Military Revolution Committee (MRC) and set the date of October 24, 1917, for the Second All-

Russia Congress of Soviets. Trotsky planned for the Congress of Soviets to endorse the overthrow of the Provisional Government. By doing this, the insurrection would appear to have the support of all of Russia.

On October 23, Kerensky became aware of the revolutionary rumblings. He ordered Lenin's arrest, calling him an enemy of the state and a German spy. Kerensky also ordered troops to make a sweep of Petrograd to find and arrest Trotsky and all members of the MRC.

## "The Provisional Government Has Fallen"

On the morning of October 24, 1917, Trotsky mobilized the MRC and the Bolsheviks to defend Petrograd. Lenin went into hiding in a working-class neighborhood, where he would remain for the rest of the day. Members of the MRC fanned out across the city and occupied government buildings, the state bank, railway depots, bridges, and telephone and telegraph stations. By 2:00 a.m. on October 25, the MRC had control of the city. In the morning, the citizens of Petrograd went about their daily routines unaware of what had occurred during the night. At 10:00 a.m., Lenin issued a statement to the All-Russia Congress of Soviets: the Provisional Government had fallen, and the Bolsheviks were in power. By evening, the Bolsheviks controlled the entire city, except the Winter Palace—the seat of the Provisional Government.

At 7:00 p.m., two men on bicycles rode up to the Winter Palace with an ultimatum. If the members of the Provisional Government did not surrender, the masses of workers would storm the palace and arrest the members. Only a small number of government ministers were inside the palace. Outside, guarding the palace, were 300 soldiers, 100 cadets, and 130 female guards known as the Women's Battalion of Death. The Provisional Government ignored the ultimatum.

At approximately 9:40 p.m., the battle cruiser *Aurora,* which had been taken over by the Bolsheviks, fired a blank shot to signal the all-out assault on the Winter Palace. Members of the MRC stormed the palace, ready to face fierce Cossack cavalrymen. However, the Cossacks provided little resistance to the Bolsheviks. Instead, they deserted their government. Some bands of the MRC entered the palace only to meet fleeing cadets and members of the Women's Battalion of Death. Unfamiliar with the vast building, some Bolsheviks entered through one door and found themselves exiting through another—and meeting fellow MRC members charging in through the same door. There was mass confusion as cadets and members of the Women's Battalion mixed with MRC fighters, but there was little resistance.

Shortly after midnight, the confusion lessened. A group of Bolsheviks entered a room in the Winter Palace, where 13 members of the Provisional Government sat

**October or November?**

Why do some sources date the Bolshevik Revolution as October 25, 1917, and others cite it as November 7, 1917?

The Julian calendar used throughout Europe had been introduced by Julius Caesar in 45 BCE. However, in 1582, Pope Gregory XIII proclaimed an updated version of the calendar, which came to be known as the Gregorian calendar. The Catholic Church was the first to adopt the new calendar. It went into effect on October 4, 1582. The next day, according to the new calendar, was October 15, 1582.

The kingdoms of Europe slowly accepted the new, more accurate Gregorian calendar. The Catholic kingdoms of Spain and Portugal (and their American colonies), France, and Italy were the first to change to the new calendar. Non-Catholic countries initially resisted. However, as the years went on, the use of different calendars caused too much confusion between countries trying to do business. The British Empire did not adopt the Gregorian calendar until 1752.

Russia was the last of the major European nations to switch calendars. On January 24, 1918, the Council of People's Commissars decreed that the date following Wednesday, January 31, 1918, would be Thursday, February 14, 1918, according to the Gregorian calendar. That is why it is possible—and correct—to say that Red October happened in November!

calmly around a large table. An MRC officer placed them under arrest. At 2:30 a.m., Lenin sent word to the chairman of the All-Russia Congress who announced that the Winter Palace had been taken. All of Russia was now under the control of the Petrograd Soviet. Lenin immediately organized a committee of Bolsheviks to govern Russia.

In Moscow, intense fighting continued as Bolsheviks struggled for control of the city. In less than a week, Moscow, too, was under the control of the Bolsheviks. The Bolsheviks were victorious. The party symbol, the red flag of socialism, waved over rooftops. The Bolshevik Revolution of 1917 would be remembered as Red October.

**Rewriting History**

For the Soviets, the storming of the Winter Palace by Bolshevik revolutionaries was their moment of glory. Unfortunately, the actual event was not impressive. Therefore, the Soviets rewrote history.

The unimpressive event was represented as a spur-of-the-moment eruption of the people's enthusiasm for the revolution. The revised version depicted tens of thousands of workers storming the palace gates. They fearlessly faced the barrels of loaded guns held by stern and hardened soldiers.

*A portion of the Winter Palace damaged by the Bolshevik Revolution*

Chapter 8

Vladimir Lenin speaking to retain support

# Civil War and the Birth of the Soviet Union

Although the Bolsheviks—the Reds—were in power in Petrograd and Moscow, much of Russia was not under their control. The first acts of the Bolshevik government included an immediate implementation of land redistribution and peace talks with Germany. The Bolshevik regime made many positive changes in Russia. These changes included the separation of church and state, the expulsion of the clergy from schools, equal rights for women, and the loss of special privileges for the hereditary nobility.

However, in the Bolsheviks' interpretation of Marxist theory, a democracy that guarantees personal freedoms would have been a step backward. According to Marx, socialism is only a stage in the revolutionary process toward a communist utopia.

His theory explains that after a capitalist regime has been overthrown, a workers' socialist regime would take over. The role of the socialist government was to see to the equal distribution of goods and services to all citizens in proportion to individual needs. All means of production—the farms and factories, etc.—would be socialized and in the hands of the government, thus making all citizens equal. People would produce exactly what was expected of them and receive only what they needed. Once society was socialized and all the wealth forcibly redistributed among the people, the government could step aside and let the communist ideal be realized.

Under communism, all people would live in harmony. Government would be unnecessary because there would be no private property, no money, no wars, and no taxes. Everything would be held in common, and people would be equal—no one would be above anyone else.

## The Beginning of a Civil War

Despite their ideas about democracy, Lenin and the Bolsheviks could not ignore the will of the people. The Russian people pressed for the formation of a Constituent Assembly that would determine the constitutional future of Russia.

On November 25, 1917, elections were held. The Bolsheviks were not pleased with the results. More than 41 million votes were cast. The Socialist-Revolutionary Party (SR) received 40 percent of the votes. The Socialist Democratic Labor Party (SD)—the Bolsheviks—received only 25 percent of the votes.

Lenin was humiliated. The Russian people had rejected his interpretation of Marxism, but he would not allow them to stand in his way. When the Constituent Assembly met for the first time to organize a democratic Russia, Lenin ordered the assembly to be closed down. There would be no

Petrograd members of a women's regiment in the army

democracy in Russia. The Russian people were called upon to stand up to Lenin and the Bolsheviks. A civil war was at hand.

## The Reds and the Whites

The Reds—the Bolsheviks—interpreted the conflict as one between workers and the bourgeois middle class, who sought to make Russia a capitalist country such as the United States or France. The Whites included various anti-Bolshevik political groups, including supporters of the tsar, liberal democrats, SRs, and Mensheviks. The Whites viewed the Civil War as a struggle for democracy against the tyranny of the Bolsheviks.

A third party also played a part in the Civil War. So-called Green armies consisted of peasants and anarchists who opposed and attacked both the Red and White forces. The Green armies wanted to protect their communities from being forced to give aid in supplies or men.

Historians, however, view the Civil War as a continuation of the October Revolution. The Bolsheviks held only Petrograd and Moscow and some farmland in between the two cities. The Germans held vast expanses of European Russia. The rest of the country was in a state of anarchy—without a government.

Trotsky had organized the workers' militias and the Military Revolution Committee (MRC) into the Red Army. They were victorious in many of the early skirmishes against the White forces. Trotsky also negotiated the Treaty of Brest-Litvosk, which was signed March 3, 1918, and formally ended Russia's involvement in World War I. This act finalized the rift between SDs and SRs. The Marxist-leaning members of the SR party left the government in protest against the peace treaty and joined the ranks of the White Army. The party of Lenin was now solely in charge. The Bolsheviks alone ruled all of Russia and moved swiftly to consolidate their power and seek an end to the Civil War. In March 1918, the Bolsheviks moved to Moscow and made it the capital of their new government—the Russian Soviet Federative Socialist Republic.

**Leon Trotsky**

Leon Trotsky was born Lev Davidovich Bronstein in Ukraine on October 26, 1879. A follower of Marxist philosophy, he joined the Socialist Democratic Party (SD). Trotsky was arrested in 1898 for organizing a workers' union and sentenced to two years in prison and four years' exile in Siberia. In 1902, he escaped and moved to London, where he became acquainted with other Russian Marxists in exile, including Vladimir Ilyich Lenin.

In 1903, Trotsky attended the Second Congress, where the split between the Bolsheviks and Mensheviks occurred. At the time, Trotsky sided with the Mensheviks, favoring a large, all-inclusive party organization. However, Trotsky disagreed with the Menshevik revolutionary tactics of supporting the liberal bourgeoisie as a step to forming a communist society.

After the revolution of 1905, Trotsky returned to Russia and led the St. Petersburg Soviet. In 1907, he was exiled again but fled to Western Europe. After the outbreak of World War I, he fled to New York, where he stayed until after the February Revolution in 1917.

After the tsar's abdication, Trotsky allied with Lenin. When Lenin went into hiding after the July Days of 1917, Trotsky assumed the Bolshevik leadership and laid the groundwork for the October Revolution.

With Russia's withdrawal from the war with Germany, British troops landed in the Baltic port cities of Arkhangel'sk and Murmansk. These troops came to protect Allied war material that had been left behind Russian lines during the war. American and Japanese armies were stationed for the same reasons in Siberia. Though their express goal was not the overthrow of the Bolsheviks, they nonetheless offered support to the anti-Bolshevik armies.

By the close of 1918, the Whites held most of southern Russia and Siberia. Although the Whites held more territory than the Reds, the areas they controlled were underdeveloped compared to the industrial corridor between Petrograd (which the Reds had retaken) and Moscow. Transportation was slow and tedious; communication lines were scarce. Wherever the White armies conquered, they tried to establish Provisional Governments.

However, these weak governments were unable to match the organization and drive of the Reds. When the Allied powers won World War I, the Allied armies of Great Britain, the United States, and Japan withdrew from Russia. This left the anti-Bolshevik armies without support. The commanders of the White armies were former tsarist generals with much battlefield experience but very few recruits.

Trotsky's Red Army was developing into a formidable fighting force. The core of the Red Army was the Red Brigade, a coalition of workers' militias from the prerevolution days. Trotsky later expanded the ranks with voluntary recruitment and, after the summer of 1918, forced military service. To lead an army of millions, Trotsky had, like the Whites, drafted tsarist officers. However, in order to ensure the loyalty of the former tsarists, the commanders' families were held hostage. One wrong order could result in the murder of a general's entire family. Furthermore, every order a military commander gave was countersigned by a Bolshevik party member. As 1919 continued, the Red Army secured more and more victories for the Bolsheviks.

**Shots!**

On August 30, 1918, an attempt was made on Lenin's life. He was in Moscow and had just finished speaking to workers at a factory. As Lenin was getting into his chauffeur-driven car, Fanya Kaplan caught his attention by asking questions. Then, several shots were fired. Two entered Lenin's shoulder, and one punctured his left lung. Lenin fell to the ground. Although Lenin survived the attempted assassination, bullets remained lodged in his body.

Fanya Kaplan was caught and taken into custody. She admitted to shooting Lenin. However, no witnesses actually saw her shoot him. Reportedly, she had a handgun in her possession, but it did not match the bullets. Was she guilty, or was she a scapegoat? Accounts of her punishment differ. Some say Kaplan was executed several days later by the Cheka, and other accounts state she was exiled to Siberia.

## The Cheka

To ensure loyalty, the Bolsheviks created a secret police called the All-Russian Extraordinary Commission for the Struggle Against Counter-Revolution, Sabotage, and Speculation. Founded in December 1917, the secret police was also known as the Cheka. Wherever the Red Army had been victorious, the Cheka followed closely behind to ensure that everyone adhered to the Bolshevik philosophy. The Cheka has been described as an "organ of terror dispensing summary justice including executions, making mass arrests, and taking hostages at random."[1]

The Cheka quickly surpassed even the tsarist secret police in its reputation for cruelty. People were shot at random, no questions asked, to instill fear in the masses and prevent any counter-revolutionary activities. In 1918, nearly 9,000 people were shot without a trial. By some estimates, the dreaded Cheka murdered as many as 50,000 Russians by the close of the Civil War in 1920. The Bolsheviks had implemented a reign of fear—the so-called Red Terror.

The Cheka was not alone in its use of terror to ensure loyalty to their cause. White Army

*The Cheka (secret police) are reviewed by their officers.*

commanders and anti-Bolshevik extremists killed, arrested, or tormented the Russian people on a level equal to, if not greater than, the Reds. Suspected communists were shot by a firing squad without trial. Thousands of communists were jailed or sent into forced labor. One of the most chilling tactics of the White Terror was the systematic harassment of Jews. These anti-Semitic mob actions, called pogroms, had been common even in tsarist Russia. Jews were often falsely blamed for crop failures, revolutions, economic recessions, and plagues. As some of the leading Bolsheviks were of Jewish descent, some Whites blamed the Jews for the problems Russia faced. They also urged villagers to raid Jewish communities, burn their homes and shops, and terrorize the residents. Thousands were murdered by angry mobs. During the Civil War in Russia, no side was innocent of brutality.

**Not Welcome**

In 1919, the Red Army was sent into Poland to "liberate" the Polish people from their "evil" bourgeois government. The Bolsheviks were shocked and horrified that the Poles greeted the Russians as invaders and not as proletarian brothers. The socialist dictatorship had a long way to go before the communist ideal could be realized.

## A Socialist Dictatorship

By 1920, the Red Army had conquered the White Army and driven many of the democrats into exile. Russia was firmly under the rule of the Bolsheviks. Lenin's attention now turned to the formation of his socialist dictatorship. Lenin stressed a strategy of War Communism—the rapid forcing of Marxist ideals on the Russian people and economy. This had begun in earnest during the Civil War. Lenin and his ministers stepped up efforts across Russia, especially in lands formerly held by the White Army, to bring about the socialist dictatorship. Private property was abolished. All industries were nationalized. Peasants, factory workers, teachers, and doctors now were all government workers.

In the countryside, the government encouraged the redistribution of land among the peasants. However, it did little in the way of organizing the process. Russian agricultural practices were still far behind those of Western Europe and North America. Production was already low—little was done to increase it. The produce of the land was often forcibly taken from the peasants for the Red Army and workers in the cities—the backbone of the Bolshevik movement. The result was a further decrease in agricultural production. By 1921, Russian farms produced one-half of what they had in 1913. Famine followed. An estimated 5 million men, women, and children died of starvation in 1921.

Meanwhile, Lenin organized all of the Russian workers' soviets under the Council of People's Commissars. As the council's chairman, he wielded an extraordinary amount of influence. Lenin had become the sole ruler in Russia. By killing or exiling those who disagreed with Lenin, the Bolsheviks had done away with all rival political parties. The party of the Bolshevik Revolution now ruled Russia.

## Union of Soviet Socialist Republics

The Bolsheviks also organized soviets in nations that had previously been part of the Russian Empire, such as Ukraine, Belarus, and the Caucasus. These "independent" socialist republics officially joined with Russia on December 28, 1922. This union of all soviets under the Communist Party and under Lenin's Council of People's Commissars created a new country, now called the Union of Soviet Socialist Republics (USSR). The USSR, a socialist empire as vast as Russia's tsarist empire, enforced Marxist ideals as interpreted by Vladimir Ilyich Lenin through a socialist dictatorship until its collapse in 1991.

FIFTEEN CENTS November 21, 1927

TIME

The Weekly Newsmagazine

Drawing by Annenkov

Volume X

L. D. TROTSKY

*He abandoned the Bronx.*

(See RUSSIA)

Number 21

*Leon Trotsky was depicted on the November 21, 1927, cover of* TIME *magazine in recognition of ten years of Bolshevik rule.*

Chapter 9

Vladimir Lenin and Joseph Stalin in 1922

# The Soviet Empire

Lenin believed the proletarian struggle was an international phenomenon, not just a Russian issue. He closely followed socialist movements around the world. In March 1919, he had declared the opening of the Third International, or Communist International (Comintern). Lenin called for a worldwide socialist revolution along the Russian model. However, a major proletarian revolution had yet to arrive in Europe.

Lenin also recognized that his plan for communism was not working. In 1921, he had initiated his New Economic Policy (NEP). This was a brief retreat from forcing socialism onto the broken Russian economic system. Under the NEP, limited private ownership was allowed, and it was met with a return of businesses and a recovery of the Soviet economy.

## Planning the Soviet Union's Future

Lenin suffered a series of strokes beginning in May 1922, and a stroke in December severely limited his abilities. Lenin began to chart the direction of the Soviet Union for others to follow after his death. Lenin favored a collective leadership, where power would be determined by the Communist Party and its chairman. He strongly opposed Joseph Stalin, the General Secretary of the Central Committee. Stalin was among the people Lenin did not want to assume the leadership. Stalin's dictatorial manner, cruelty, and his preference for a huge bureaucracy clashed with Lenin's ideas. Lenin died of a fatal stroke in January 1924. Leon Trotsky and Joseph Stalin struggled briefly, but bitterly, for control. Stalin emerged as victor.

## Stalinism

Joseph Stalin ruled with an iron fist. In 1928, he renounced Lenin's NEP and embarked on a long and difficult—though successful—plan of rapid industrialization. Stalin harnessed the energies of the nation's large population and its immense natural resources. He transformed the Soviet Union from a chiefly agricultural society to a modern, heavily industrialized military machine. Soviet factories pounded out tons of steel, iron,

### Workers of the World, Unite!

Lenin believed that the revolt of the proletariat against the bourgeoisie was not a matter of national politics but an international movement. In March 1919, Lenin organized the Third International, commonly referred to as the Comintern, or the Communist International. The Comintern's goal was to organize a worldwide proletariat revolution, much like Russia's. Its rallying cry was: Workers of the World, Unite!

The Comintern dwindled after Lenin's death as conditions improved for workers across Europe. However, Joseph Stalin reorganized the Comintern for his own purposes. He used it not as an agent for worldwide communist revolution but rather as an international web of Soviet spies and secret agents.

railroad equipment, farm machinery, machine tools, airplanes, and tanks. A complex set of railway lines were built and networked the Eurasian continent.

Stalin created Five-Year Plans that brought all industries under the control of the state. The plans determined what, where, and how much of the country's manufactured goods were to be produced. But this boom in development came at a huge cost in human misery and environmental disaster. Those who expressed even the slightest doubt about Stalin's Five-Year Plans were subject to police brutality and long sentences in Siberian slave-labor camps.

As Stalin rushed to bring all the farms under the government's complete control, an estimated 7 million people died from famine. Stalin moved the people out of the villages and into vast apartment complexes with communal dining halls. No one family worked one plot of land. Everyone was forced to work vast tracts of land together.

The sense of closeness to the land and the sense of pride in one's work became lost in Stalin's modernizations. Peasants toiled the entire year only to watch as their harvest was packed up and taken away. In time, morale dropped and peasants refused to work. Some farmers chose to set their crops on fire rather than see them confiscated by armed guards. Agricultural production continued to decrease. Stalin's response was not to change his concept but to punish the peasants. In the 1930s, Stalin began the first of his great "purges." People accused of harboring doubts about Stalin's policies were sent to Siberian labor camps without trial.

**A Worker's Life**

Industrial laborers worked long, hard hours in conditions that were often dangerous.

The pay was poor, and there was little they could spend it on. Nevertheless, many believed in Stalin, his promises, and the ideals of communism.

Propaganda in the form of pamphlets and posters constantly reminded workers that communism would lead to utopia. Fear tactics also played a part. Workers' pay was dependent not only on personal production but also on the production of others in their group.

## A Pact with Hitler

In 1938, Great Britain, France, and the United States feared the emerging power of Nazi Germany. They held a number of secret meetings with the USSR about restraining Adolf Hitler. However, on August 23, 1939, Joseph Stalin shocked the world by signing a nonaggression pact with Hitler. According to the agreement, neither Germany nor the Soviet Union would turn its military on the other, despite what may happen in the rest of the world.

German infantry near Moscow during their invasion of the Soviet Union in World War II

On September 1, 1939, Germany invaded Poland, and World War II broke out across Europe. Then, in mid-1940, Hitler broke his pact with Stalin and began making plans to invade the Soviet Union. On June 22, 1941, Germany invaded the Soviet Union. In December 1941, the United States, Great Britain, and the Soviet Union became military allies against Hitler's Germany. On April 24, 1945, the Red Army encircled Hitler's capital, Berlin, bringing about the end of World War II in Europe.

## The Iron Curtain

Despite a Soviet victory, the losses were tremendous. Millions of people had lost their lives in what Stalin called "the Great Patriotic War." After the defeat of Hitler, Germany was divided up among the Allied victors: the United States, the United Kingdom, France, and the USSR. The Soviets took control of East Germany and consolidated its Eastern European empire.

In late 1946, Britain's Winston Churchill remarked that an "iron curtain" was descending over Central and Eastern Europe. Marxist ideology was forced on the occupied countries and incorporated into the Eastern Bloc.

The United States was determined to help revive the devastated European economy through capitalist ventures, but the Soviet Union remained committed to the international proletarian struggle. The Soviets and the Americans could not reconcile their vastly different political and economic differences. During the next 50 years, the two greatest powers in the world, the USSR and the United States, would face off in a cold war of ideological differences.

## New Leaders and the Cold War

In March 1953, Joseph Stalin died. Nikita Khrushchev succeeded Stalin. Khrushchev initiated a vast "de-Stalinization" program aimed at reviving the economy and earning the people's trust.

During Khrushchev's era, the USSR and the United States had vastly expanded their arsenals of nuclear weapons. Khrushchev and U.S. President John F. Kennedy confronted each other during the terrifying Cuban Missile Crisis of 1962. The two superpowers were brought to the brink of nuclear holocaust.

From 1964 to 1985, Soviet leaders Leonid Brezhnev, Yuri Andropov, and Konstantin Chernenko continued the cold war with the United States. Each ruled over a relatively stable USSR.

In 1985, Mikhail Gorbachev came to power. Striving to reform the Soviet Union, Gorbachev ushered in a period of *glasnost* (openness) and *perestroika* (economic reconstruction). He aimed to increase the economic growth of the Soviet Union. He also tried to open up the government and

**A Man of Steel**

Joseph Stalin was born December 18, 1878. Between the years of 1902 and 1913, he was arrested and exiled to Siberia eight times. While in prison, he changed his name to Stalin, which means "man of steel." He was able to escape prison seven times.

permit a freer society. Gorbachev worked to warm relations with the United States.

The Soviet satellite countries of Eastern Europe began to demand freedom from Soviet domination and the "dictatorship of the proletariat." In 1989, the Berlin Wall, which had been built to separate Communist East Germany from West Germany, came down amid mass demonstrations. The Soviet Union began to crumble, too.

On June 12, 1991, Boris Yeltsin became the first elected president of the Union of Soviet Socialist Republics. On December 8, 1991, President Yeltsin signed the Belavezha Accords, officially dismantling the Union of Soviet Socialist Republics. After 74 years, Lenin's Bolshevik Revolution had ended.

*Boris Yeltsin served as Russia's first elected president from 1991 to 1999.*

# Timeline

| 1904 | 1905 | 1905 |
|---|---|---|
| The Russo-Japanese War begins. | On January 9 (Bloody Sunday), 130 people are killed and several hundred people are wounded. | Tsar Nicholas II calls for an Imperial Duma in August. |

| 1914 | 1916 | 1917 |
|---|---|---|
| Russia goes to war against Germany in July. | Rasputin is murdered by noblemen in December. | The February Revolution occurs and places the Bolsheviks in power. |

| 1905 | 1905 | 1905 |
|---|---|---|
| Treaty of Portsmouth is signed on September 5, ending the Russo-Japanese War. | The St. Petersburg Soviet is founded in October. | October Manifesto is signed by Nicholas II on October 17. |

| 1917 | 1917 | 1917 |
|---|---|---|
| Tsar Nicholas II abdicates on March 15. | July Days demonstrations are held. | The General Kornilov coup attempt occurs in late August. |

# Timeline

| 1917 | 1918 | 1919 |
|---|---|---|
| Bolsheviks storm the Winter Palace and topple the Provisional Government on October 24 and 25. | The Romanovs are murdered in Ekaterinburg on July 16 and 17. | The Red Army routs the White Army in Siberia in November. |

| 1939 | 1939 | 1945 |
|---|---|---|
| Stalin signs a non-aggression pact on August 23 with Adolf Hitler. | Hitler invades Poland on September 1. | The Red Army surrounds Berlin on April 24. |

| 1921 | 1924 | 1928 |
|---|---|---|
| Lenin initiates the New Economic Policy (NEP) in March. | Vladimir Ilyich Lenin dies in January. | Stalin rejects the NEP and begins massive industrialization and modernization programs. |

| 1962 | 1989 | 1991 |
|---|---|---|
| The Cuban Missile Crisis begins on October 14. | The Berlin Wall begins to come down on November 9. | An agreement is signed that dissolves the Union of Soviet Socialist Republics on December 8. |

# Essential Facts

## Date of Event

October 25, 1917

## Place of Event

Petrograd (St. Petersburg), Russia

## Key Players

- Tsar Nicholas II
- Vladimir Ilyich Lenin
- Leon Trotsky
- Alexander Kerensky

## Highlights of Event

- The October Manifesto of 1905 promised social and political reform.
- Russia's 1914 entry into World War I resulted in general dissatisfaction.
- The Russian people overthrew their absolute monarch, Tsar Nicholas II, in February 1917.
- In April 1917, Lenin demanded that no Russians support the Provisional Government. Rather, they should push for a dictatorship of the proletariat.

- The Russian people marched in protest in July 1917 against the continuing war and in anger over the failings of the Provisional Government.
- Lenin instigated a coup against the Provisional Government in October 1917.
- Tsar Nicholas II, his family, and servants were murdered July 16 and 17, 1918. Their bodies were hidden by the Bolshevik secret police, the Cheka.
- The Civil War raged across Russia from 1918 to 1920 as Lenin's Bolsheviks (the Reds) fought against the White Army.
- The Union of Soviet Socialist Republics (USSR) was formed December 28, 1922. The Bolshevik-founded, communist USSR ruled Russia and much of Eastern Europe until its eventual collapse in 1991.

## Quote

"Society as a whole is more and more splitting up into two great hostile camps, into two great classes directly facing each other: Bourgeoisie and Proletariat."—*Karl Marx and Friedrich Engels,* The Communist Manifesto

# Additional Resources

## Select Bibliography

Daniels, Robert V. *Red October: The Bolshevik Revolution of 1917*. New York: Charles Scribner's Sons, 1970.

Massie, Robert K. *The Romanovs: The Final Chapter*. New York: Random House, 1995.

Mawdsley, Evan. *The Russian Civil War*. New York: Pegasus, 2007.

Pipes, Richard. *A Concise History of the Russian Revolution*. New York: Alfred A. Knopf, 1995.

## Further Reading

Dunn, John M. *The Russian Revolution*. San Diego, CA: Lucent Books, 1996.

Haney, John. *Vladimir Ilyich Lenin*. New York: Chelsea House Books, 1988.

Matthews, John. *The Rise and Fall of the Soviet Union*. San Diego, CA: Lucent Books, 2000.

## Web Links

To learn more about the Bolshevik Revolution, visit ABDO Publishing Company online at **www.abdopublishing.com**. Web sites about the Bolshevik Revolution are featured on our Book Links page. These links are routinely monitored and updated to provide the most current information available.

## Places to Visit

**Armoury Chamber of the Kremlin Museum**
Moscow, Russia
www.kremlin.museum.ru/en/main/museums/armoury
What was once the tsars' weapons storehouse now displays coronation robes, royal carriages, and jewels. The Armoury, the Kremlin's main museum, holds an impressive collection of armor and weaponry.

**Museum of Russian Art**
5500 Stevens Avenue South, Minneapolis, MN 55419
612-821-9045
www.tmora.org
Presently, this is the only nonprofit museum in North America dedicated to educational exhibitions and related events pertaining to Russian art and artifacts from the nineteenth and twentieth centuries.

**Russian Cultural Centre**
1825 Phelps Place Northwest, Washington, DC 20008
202-265-3840
www.rccusa.org
The Russian Cultural Centre is affiliated with the Russian Foreign Ministry. A variety of exhibits and presentations on Russian culture are offered.

# Glossary

**agrarian**
Related to farming and agricultural interests.

**autocratic**
Related to a form of government in which a ruler has absolute power and authority.

**capitalism**
An economic system in which the means of production are privately owned and operated for profit and not solely for the benefit of the state or community.

**caste**
A category within a rigid social system in which individuals are grouped by wealth, rank, or occupation.

**Cheka**
Secret police organized by Lenin to eliminate resistance to the Bolshevik Revolution.

**communism**
An ideology that seeks a classless and stateless utopian society based on equality and communal ownership of property.

**Constituent Assembly**
A body elected for the sole purpose of determining and drafting a nation's constitution.

**coup**
The overthrow of an existing government.

**hemophilia**
A blood disorder that results in potentially fatal bleeding from cuts or bruises.

**insurrection**
A revolt against an authority or system of government.

**intelligentsia**
A social class of intellectuals in Russia concerned with social and political change.

**Leningrad**

The name given to Petrograd (St. Petersburg) after the death of Vladimir Ilyich Lenin in 1924.

**liberal democracy**

A system of government in which leaders and representatives are selected by the people. It is bound by the rule of law and obliged to protect the rights and liberties of its citizens.

**Marxism**

The theory and practice of the philosophy of Karl Marx as applied to history, economics, and politics.

**Military Revolutionary Committee (MRC)**

An armed militia organized by the workers' soviets during the Bolshevik Revolution. Members of the MRC became the nucleus of the Red Army.

**pseudonym**

A false or fictitious name.

**republic**

A form of government led by elected individuals.

**socialism**

A system in which the government or community controls goods and services for the equal distribution of wealth among citizens.

**soviet**

A local council of workers, soldiers, or peasants.

**tsar**

Derived from the Roman name *Caesar*, the family name of the Roman emperors. It is the title of the emperors of Russia.

**utopia**

A place of ideal perfection—especially regarding government and social conditions.

**Winter Palace**

The official residence of the royal family in St. Petersburg and later the seat of the Provisional Government.

# Source Notes

**Chapter 1. The End of a Dynasty**
1. Robert K. Massie. *The Romanovs: The Final Chapter*. New York: Random House, 1995. 4.
2. Ibid. 5.

**Chapter 2. The Old Regime**
None

**Chapter 3. New Ideas**
1. Karl Marx and Friedrich Engels. *The Communist Manifesto*. New York: Penguin Classics, 1986. 79–80.

**Chapter 4. Lenin and the Bolsheviks**
None

**Chapter 5. World War I and the Russian Revolution**
1. Richard Pipes. *A Concise History of the Russian Revolution*. New York: Alfred A. Knopf, 1995. 283.
2. Winston S. Churchill. *Maxims and Reflections*. White Fish, MT: Kessinger Publishing, 2005. 48.

**Chapter 6. The *April Theses* and July Days**

1. Vladimir Lenin. *April Theses*. 2 Jan. 2002. First World War.com. 10 Dec. 2007 <http://www.firstworldwar.com/source/apriltheses.htm>.

**Chapter 7. Red October**

None

**Chapter 8. Civil War and the Birth of the Soviet Union**

1. Sheila Fitzpatrick. *The Russian Revolution*. London: Oxford University Press, 1982. 76.

**Chapter 9. The Soviet Empire**

None

# Index

## Index Continued

## About the Author

Joseph R. O'Neill is a historian, author, and freelance journalist living in Los Angeles, California. He holds a BA in classics and history from Monmouth College, Illinois, and an MA in ancient history from the University of Illinois. He has also studied at the University of Toronto, Canada, and the American School of Classical Studies at Athens, Greece. He has written several books and articles on a range of historical and literary topics and was a contributing author for the *Encyclopedia of the Ancient Greek World* (2006).

## Photo Credits

Bridgeman Art Library/Isaak Israilevich Brodsky, cover; AP Images, 6, 10, 13, 14, 21, 46, 49, 66, 72, 81, 86, 91; Bettmann/Corbis/ Sergei Mikhailovich Prokudin-Gorskii, 23; Getty Images, 24, 56, 62; Bridgeman Art Library/Vladimir Egorovich Makovsky, 28; AP Images/Matthias Rietschel, 37; Swim Ink/Corbis, 38; Getty Images/Ivan Shagin, 45; Time & Life Pictures/Getty Images, 55, 85; Bettmann/Corbis, 65, 71; Corbis, 75; AP Images/Boris Yurchenko, 95